WHEN DANGER HITS HOME:

Survivors of Domestic Violence

WHEN DANGER HITS HOME:

Survivors of Domestic Violence

Joyce Zoldak

Mason Crest Publishers

WHEN DANGER HITS HOME:
Survivors of Domestic Violence

MASON CREST PUBLISHERS INC.
370 Reed Road
Broomall, Pennsylvania 19008
(866)MCP-BOOK (toll free)
www.masoncrest.com

Because the stories in this series are told by real people, in some cases names have been changed to protect the privacy of the individuals.

First Printing
9 8 7 6 5 4 3 2 1
ISBN 978-1-4222-0449-8 (series)
ISBN 978-1-4222-1462-6 (series) (pbk.)

Library of Congress Cataloging-in-Publication Data

Zoldak, Joyce.
  When danger hits home : survivors of domestic violence /
Joyce Zoldak. —
1st printing.
      p. cm. — (Survivors: ordinary people, extraordinary circumstances)
  Includes bibliographical references and index.
  ISBN 978-1-4222-0460-3 (alk. paper)
  Paperback ISBN 978-1-4222-1473-2 (pbk.)
  1. Family violence—United States—Juvenile literature.
  2. Family violence—United States—Prevention—Juvenile literature. I. Title.
  HV6626.2.Z65 2009
  362.82′920973—dc22
                                    2008023318

Design by MK Bassett-Harvey.
Produced by Harding House Publishing Service, Inc.
www.hardinghousepages.com
Cover design by Wendy Arakawa.
Printed in The Hashimite Kingdom of Jordan.

CO...

Introduction

Each of us is confronted with challenges and hardships in our daily lives. Some of us, however, have faced extraordinary challenges and severe adversity. Those who have lived—and often thrived—through affliction, illness, pain, tragedy, cruelty, fear, and even near-death experiences are known as survivors. We have much to learn from survivors and much to admire.

Survivors fascinate us. Notice how many books, movies, and television shows focus on individuals facing—and overcoming—extreme situations. *Robinson Crusoe* is probably the earliest example of this, followed by books like the *Swiss Family Robinson*. Even the old comedy *Gilligan's Island* appealed to this fascination, and today we have everything from the Tom Hanks' movie *Castaway* to the hit reality show *Survivor* and the popular TV show *Lost*.

What is it about survivors that appeals so much to us? Perhaps it's the message of hope they give us. These people have endured extreme challenges—and they've overcome them. They're ordinary people who faced extraordinary situations. And if they can do it, just maybe we can too.

This message is an appropriate one for young adults. After all, adolescence is a time of daily challenges. Change is everywhere in their lives, demanding that they adapt and cope with a constantly shifting reality. Their bodies change in response to increasing levels of sex hormones; their thinking processes change as their brains develop, allowing them to think in more abstract ways; their social lives change as new people and peers become more important. Suddenly, they experience the burning need to form their own identities. At the same time, their emotions are labile and unpredictable. The people they were as children may seem to have disappeared beneath the onslaught of new emotions, thoughts, and sensations. Young adults have to deal with every single one of these changes, all at the same time. Like many of the survivors whose stories are told in this series, adolescents' reality is often a frightening, confusing, and unfamiliar place.

Young adults are in crises that are no less real simply because these are crises we all live through (and most of us survive!) Like all survivors, young adults emerge from their crises transformed; they are not the people they were before. Many of them bear scars they will carry with them for life—and yet these scars can be integrated into their new identities. Scars may even become sources of strength.

In this book series, young adults will have opportunities to learn from individuals faced with tremendous struggles. Each individual has her own story, her own set of circumstances and challenges, and her own way of coping and surviving. Whether facing cancer or abuse, terrorism or natural disaster, genocide or school violence, all the survivors who tell their stories in this series have found the ability and will to carry on despite the trauma. They cope, persevere, persist, and live on as a person changed forever by the ordeal and suffering they endured. They offer hope and wisdom to young adults: if these people can do it, so can they!

These books offer a broad perspective on life and its challenges. They will allow young readers to become more self-aware of the demanding and difficult situations in their own lives—while at the same time becoming more compassionate toward those who have gone through the unthinkable traumas that occur in our world.

— Andrew M. Kleiman, M.D.

Chapter One

THE TRUTH ABOUT DOMESTIC ABUSE

S urvivors of domestic abuse all look the same. They are all middle-aged, poor, minority women with black eyes and missing teeth. Domestic abusers all look the same, too. They are all drunks who wear white tank-top undershirts and beat their wives. Right?

Wrong. Abuse comes in all shapes and sizes.

THE MANY SHAPES OF DOMESTIC ABUSE

According to K.J. Wilson in *When Violence Begins at Home,*

> If anything is truly equal opportunity, it is battering. Domestic violence crosses

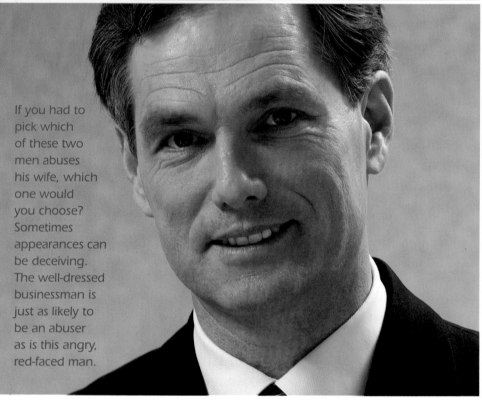

If you had to pick which of these two men abuses his wife, which one would you choose? Sometimes appearances can be deceiving. The well-dressed businessman is just as likely to be an abuser as is this angry, red-faced man.

all socioeconomic, ethnic, racial, educational, age, and religious lines.

Still, many people would prefer to believe that domestic abuse does not exist in their world. Some like to think that domestic abuse is the stuff of trailer parks or the projects. The truth is, however, that domestic abuse is a worldwide problem that cuts across social boundary lines. The forms it takes are also varied—and no one is ever completely immune. It can happen to men, women, children, teenagers, elders, heterosexuals, homosexuals, transsexuals, executives, stay-at-home moms, black people, white people,

One woman out of every three around the world has been abused in some way.

Hispanic people, Asian people, rich people, poor people, city people, country people. The popular young man who graduates valedictorian of his class with an athletic college scholarship is just as likely to be abused at

home as the overweight outcast who skips class and sits alone at lunch. The successful, confident business woman is as likely to be beaten by her husband as that lady in a scarf and rubber boots you see shuffling along the sidewalk. And a tough-as-nails retired military captain is just as apt to be abused by his caregiver as a frail, aging housewife. Domestic abuse is not picky. It can happen to anyone, anywhere, at any time.

However, one characteristic may make you more susceptible to abuse: being female. Women are the most common victims of domestic abuse worldwide. In an essay titled "Violence Against Women in the United States Is a Serious Problem," Brittney Nichols notes that, "by the most conservative estimates, one million women in the United States suffer nonfatal violence by a spouse or partner each year" and "globally, one in three women have been beaten, coerced into sex, or otherwise abused in her lifetime." While these numbers are staggering, they are only an estimate; most incidents of domestic abuse go unreported.

Although we'd all rather think that the land of domestic abuse is far, far away, chances are you know someone who has been abused, or is being abused right now. It may be someone you love, someone you hate, someone you respect, someone you're related to, someone you hardly know—or it could be the person staring back at you in the mirror.

WHAT IS DOMESTIC ABUSE?

In our quick-to-sue world, the word "abuse" itself has often been abused. Is a child who is spanked by her mother a victim of abuse? Is a wife who screams an insult at her husband in the midst of a fight being verbally abusive? If an adult child leaves his elderly mother alone while he travels for work, is he guilty of abuse? These are complicated issues, and the answers aren't always easy to determine.

The term "domestic abuse" is sometimes used interchangeably with "domestic violence," "intimate partner abuse," or "intimate partner violence." Essentially, all these terms mean the same thing: someone is the victim of calculated physical, psychological, or sexual abuse.

Physical Abuse

Physical abuse is when one person causes physical harm to another, or uses authority to threaten or intimidate a victim. Examples of physical abuse include (but are not limited to) being punched, slapped, choked, bitten, shoved, kicked, burnt, stabbed, held down, or murdered. Physical abuse also includes physical threats. For example, the abuser may punch through the wall near the victim's head or throw objects near the victim. Physical abuse also includes the confiscation of personal items, stalking, and barring exits. Some abusers use physical abuse frequently, others occasionally. Others still, never lift a

pinkie against their victims and rely solely on psychological techniques.

Even if the blow never falls on this woman, this sort of physical threat and intimidation is still considered abuse.

Psychological Abuse

Psychological abuse (also known as emotional abuse) is probably the most difficult to define, and also the most difficult to spot. According to K. J. Wilson in *When Violence Begins at Home*, "emotional abuse is any use of words, voice, action, or lack of action meant to control, hurt or demean another person."

Even if a child is provided with adequate food and never abused with physical or verbal violence, he may still be experiencing abuse in the form of neglect.

Warning Signs

It's impossible to know what goes on behind closed doors, but there are some signs and symptoms of domestic violence and abuse. If you witness a number of warning signs in a friend, family member, or co-worker, you can reasonably suspect domestic abuse.

- frequent injuries, with the excuse of "accidents"
- frequent and often unexplained absences from work or school
- frequent, harassing phone calls from the partner/parent
- fear of the partner/parent, along with references to the person's anger
- personality changes
- excessive fear of conflict
- submissive behavior, lack of assertiveness
- isolation from friends and family
- not enough resources to live (lack of money, food, transportation)
- depression, crying, low self-esteem

Examples of emotional abuse include threats, public humiliation, insults, jealous rages, accusations of **infidelity**, and isolation from friends and family. Emotional abuse isn't, however, getting into an argument with your parent or partner. Not all emotionally abused victims are physically abused, but *all* physically abused victims are emotionally abused. It is the most common, and some victims say, the most permanent form of abuse.

Emotional or psychological abuse can also include neglect. In the case of child abuse, neglect is one of the most common forms of abuse. Neglect may include a parent or guardian leaving a child home alone for long

infidelity:
marital unfaithfulness.

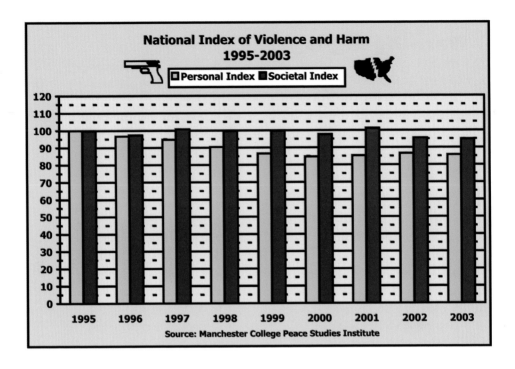

National Index of Violence and Harm
1995-2003

□ Personal Index ■ Societal Index

Source: Manchester College Peace Studies Institute

We live in a violent world. This graph shows that the incidence of "personal" (or domestic) violence is nearly as great as that of societal violence.

periods of time, often going away on long trips, regularly forgetting to pick a child up from school, or not playing an active role in a child's schoolwork or general well-being.

Sexual Abuse

Sexual abuse often goes hand-in-hand with other forms of abuse. According to the United Nations Population Fund's 2007 population-based study, "In 1 of 4 cases of domestic violence, women will also experience sexual abuse." For many abusers, sexual abuse is just one more way to induce fear and humiliation, and ultimately control their victims. Examples of sexual abuse include when someone forces another person to have sex or engage in sexual activity against his or her

According to the Women's Health section of the U.S. Department of Health and Human Services Web site (www.4woman.gov/violence), if you or someone you know has experienced any ONE of the following, you should call the National Violence Hotline at 1-800-799-7233. Remember, just ONE of these means you should make that call!

- Your partner always wants to know where you are and what you are doing.
- Your partner, guardian, or caregiver controls your finances, including withholding your own money from you or keeping track of the way you spend your own money.
- Your partner, guardian, or caregiver purposefully humiliates you in public.
- Your partner, guardian, or caregiver becomes angry or violent when he or she uses drugs or alcohol.
- Your partner, guardian, or caregiver forces you to engage in sexual activity against your will.
- Your partner, guardian, or caregiver constantly criticizes you, finding fault in everything you do.
- Your partner, guardian, or caregiver does not want you to be in contact with your friends or family.
- Your partner, guardian, or caregiver does not allow you to take the medications required by your doctor.
- Your partner, guardian, or caregiver physically abuses you or threatens to.
- Your partner falsely accuses you of cheating all the time.
- Your partner, guardian, or caregiver pressures you to quit school, your job, or other things that are important to you.
- Your partner, guardian, or caregiver abuses, or threatens to abuse, your children or your pets.
- Your partner, guardian, or caregiver breaks, disposes of, or otherwise harms things that are important to you.
- Your partner, guardian, or caregiver blames you when he or she abuses you.
- Your partner, guardian, or caregiver often neglects you.

will, when someone touches someone against his or her will, when someone exposes him- or herself, when someone forces another person to watch or look at pornography, when someone forces another person to dress in a way that makes that person uncomfortable, when someone talks to another person in a sexual way that makes that person uncomfortable, or when someone is openly unfaithful to a spouse or partner as a form of punishment. Sexual abuse can happen between married couples and between relatives. Any sexual actions that are unwelcome are wrong, no matter who does them.

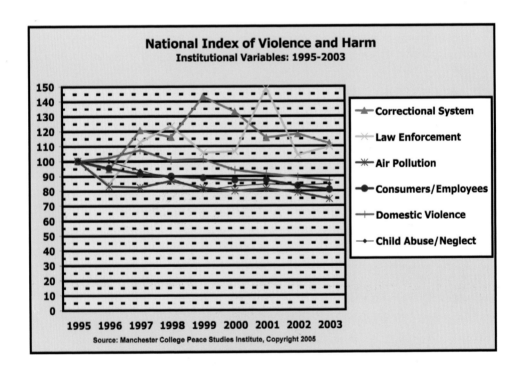

Why Do Some People Become Abusers?

Unfortunately, the answer to this question is still not fully known, and like many aspects of human nature, it may never be completely understood.

Some researchers cite substance abuse as playing a major role in abusive tendencies. We may all have angry, violent tendencies, but most of us control them; drugs and alcohol, however, diminish our inhibitions. They allow us to cross lines we might never otherwise cross.

Other researchers believe that those who were raised in abusive households are more likely to become abusive adults. Most of us have caught ourselves acting like our parents in ways that may take us by surprise. Children imitate what they grow up seeing—and the more you see violence as being an ordinary part of daily life, the more acceptable it will seem to you. Besides, children who bear the emotional scars left by abuse may grow up without the same coping mechanisms that other individuals have when it comes to handling anger and frustration.

A COMPLICATED PROBLEM

There are so many different forms of abuse that sometimes it's hard to know what is just petty fighting, and what is simply over the line. As Elaine Weiss points out in *Family and Friends' Guide to Domestic Violence*, "not every match made in hell is an abusive relationship." Sometimes people fight, argue with one another, or say things that are hurtful to one another. We all do it and it is part of existing in a world full of people who don't always get along with each other. This is not abuse. This is life. Abuse, on the other hand, is intentional and repetitive with one goal in mind. As Weiss explains:

> There are certainly bad relationships out there. . . . Then there are relationships where one partner [or person] uses a combination of physical, sexual, and psychological tactics to gain complete control over the other. The victims in these relationships live in constant fear of saying or doing the wrong thing. These are the true abusive relationships.

"That couldn't happen to me!" is the kind of thinking that sometimes gets people in trouble. Victims of domestic abuse may actually be unaware of what they're experiencing; for them, it may seem "normal." Of course, some survivors of domestic abuse knew for many years that they were being abused; it just took them time and courage to get out of their bad situations. Others, however, did not know that they were victims of domestic abuse until decades after they had left their abusers.

Abuse is a complicated thing. Sometimes it is simply more difficult to see what is right in front of your eyes. Have you ever run around the house like a crazy person, searching for a pair of eyeglasses or sunglasses—only to have someone walk in and point out that the glasses were already on your face? That's a little like the way things are for a victim of abuse: an onlooker might easily spot the

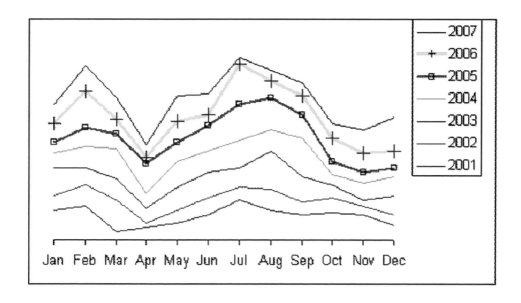

abuse that's going on—but for the person who's living in that situation, it may not be anywhere near as obvious.

How do you know for sure if you or someone you know is being abused?

Well, being sure is not the important part—getting help is. If you even so much as suspect that you or someone you know is being abused, you should talk to someone you trust. At the end of this book is a list of organizations and hotlines where you can go for more information. If you or someone you know is in immediate danger, call 911 right away.

This graph from the police department of Monterey, California, indicates that the incidence of domestic violence may rise and fall, depending on the season of the year.

WHY DON'T VICTIMS GET HELP?

If the abuser is not willing to admit the problem and take steps to change, then the victim must takes steps to protect him- or herself. This is often harder than it sounds. People who have never experienced domestic abuse themselves may wonder what makes victims of abuse stay with their abusers. The answers are complicated, and they vary with each individual case. Escaping domestic abuse is seldom as simple as just dumping the jerk who did it. Sometimes this "jerk" is someone you love, someone you trust, or your own parent or child. These relationships are so interwoven with love and need that simply walking away may not seem possible. What's more, domestic abuse is often a carefully crafted combination of tactics used to break a person down. Sometimes the abuse can be so subtle that no one realizes it until it is too late.

Elaine Weiss, a domestic violence educator and the author of *Family and Friends' Guide to Domestic Abuse* and *Surviving Domestic Violence: Voices of Women Who Broke Free* (and also a domestic abuse survivor herself), has spoken to hundreds of women about their experiences. She found that while each story was unique to the individual, certain patterns of abuse ran through all the stories. Repeating patterns also appeared in the reasons why some victims stay with their abusers, sometimes for decades.

Isolation and Self-Doubt

Think about a time when someone you trusted betrayed you. Maybe you were feeling sad or scared, and your best friend made

fun of you. Or think about the thing you dislike most about yourself, and then imagine someone you love making fun of that thing, over and over. It hurts much more when a friend betrays you than a stranger. Your friends and your family know your darkest secrets—and they know exactly what buttons to push to upset you. And when a friend or family member insults you, sometimes it's harder to laugh off their words or put them out of your mind. After all, they know you better than anyone. *Maybe they're right*, whispers a little voice inside your head.

Women who are abused may feel as though they live in an isolated world. Without realistic, objective feedback, they often doubt themselves and begin to believe the messages their abusers feed them about their self-worth and culpability.

Now take these normal feelings that we've all felt at one time or another with our friends and family, and subtract everyone else from your life except this one person who always puts you down. There are no other voices to balance this person's voice; no one to whom you can turn to complain or vent or seek another opinion. Pretty soon it becomes harder and harder not to believe this person, because his (or her) voice is the only one you're hearing.

Abusers often make sure that their victims' ties to friends and family have been severed. After all, abusers don't want anyone interfering with their control over their victims. They may not let their victims talk on the phone, visit friends, or even go to work. Eventually, the abusers' victims have little or no contact with the outside world. The only people left in their world are their abusers. The abusers' opinions are the only ones their victims' know, and their opinions seem like the truth. After all, it's their word against . . . well, no one's. Even the most self-confident person in the world could begin to doubt herself under such extreme conditions. This is one reason that many people stay in an abusive relationship for months, years, or sometimes decades.

Fear

According to Elaine Weiss, many victims stay with their abusers because they're afraid to

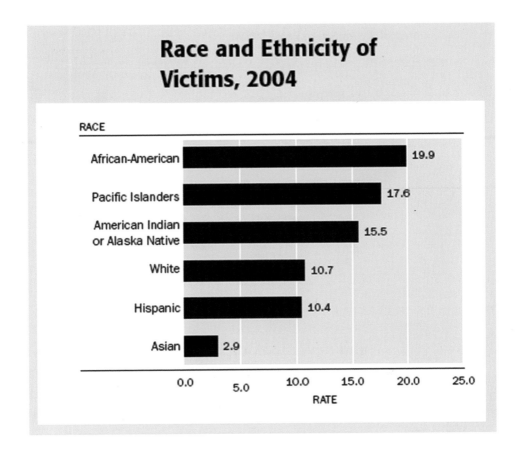

Race and Ethnicity of Victims, 2004

RACE

	RATE
African-American	19.9
Pacific Islanders	17.6
American Indian or Alaska Native	15.5
White	10.7
Hispanic	10.4
Asian	2.9

RATE

leave. People who have never experienced domestic abuse sometimes say, "Well, just fight back—or walk away!" However, most domestic abusers are men who are physically stronger than the women they abuse. In the case of elder abuse, the victims' frail condition may limit their being able to defend themselves. When a child is being abused, the adult guardian is far more imposing—both physically and psychologically—than the victim.

Leaving a domestically abusive situation is never as simple as just walking out the door

According to the U.S. Department of Health & Human Services, victims of domestic abuse are most apt to be African American. This does not necessarily mean, however, that their abusers are also African American.

Map of Victimization Rates, 2004

VICTIMS PER 1,000 CHILDREN ▨ 0.0 to 5.0 ▧ 5.1 to 10.0 ▪ 10.1 to 15.0 ▨ 15.1 to 20.0 ▪ 20.1 and greater ▢ data not available

This map from the U.S. government indicates that child abuse may occur far more frequently in some states than others.

and never looking back. According to Weiss, in cases of spousal abuse, "A woman is at most risk of being seriously injured or killed in the six months *after* she leaves than at any other time in the relationship." When abusers sense that they have lost control of their victims, they often resort to even greater violence—and abusers who have never resorted to physical violence before, may become physically abusive if their victims attempt to leave.

Spouses and partners experiencing abuse may be afraid to leave because of the effect on children in the household. Sometimes mothers believe that breaking up the family would be detrimental to their children. Others depend financially on their abusers and fear they would not be able to provide for their children if they left. Many wives

depend on their spouses for health insurance for themselves and their children—and some mothers would rather take a beating than make their children potentially homeless and without adequate healthcare. What many victims don't realize, however, is that children who are raised in a domestically abusive household are in more danger the longer they remain in the home. Witnessing abuse is emotionally damaging to the children as well; and those who physically

Domestic abuse is not always visible to outsiders looking in at a family. Sometimes even families that appear to be happy and loving may hide secrets.

Neglect is the most common form of child abuse.

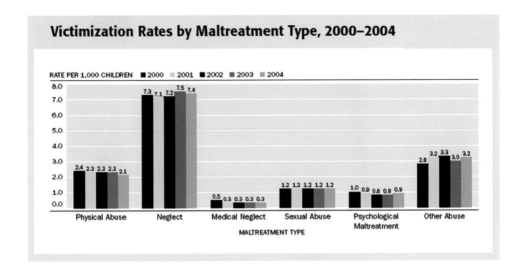

Victimization Rates by Maltreatment Type, 2000–2004

RATE PER 1,000 CHILDREN ■ 2000 ▢ 2001 ■ 2002 ■ 2003 ▨ 2004

Physical Abuse: 2.4 2.3 2.3 2.3 2.1
Neglect: 7.3 7.1 7.2 7.5 7.4
Medical Neglect: 0.5 0.3 0.3 0.3 0.3
Sexual Abuse: 1.2 1.2 1.2 1.2 1.2
Psychological Maltreatment: 1.0 0.9 0.8 0.8 0.9
Other Abuse: 2.8 3.2 3.3 3.0 3.2

MALTREATMENT TYPE

abuse their spouse or partner are more likely to physically abuse their children. Many people in domestically abusive situations do not realize that the long-term effects of being raised in abusive households are more detrimental to children's well-being than leaving—and there are community resources and shelters that can help victims and their children escape.

Religion

Some religions frown on divorce or the break-up of the nuclear family. Studies show that women with deep religious beliefs tend to stay in abusive relationships longer than women who are not religious; these women would rather endure the abuse than go against what they believe to be the grain of their religion. In reality, however, according to Weiss, "There is no major religion that

Children can be the victims of domestic abuse directly—but they can also suffer because they live in a family where abuse is taking place between other members of the household.

Are Abusers Evil?

Anyone can find himself or herself in an abusive situation—and most of us could also find ourselves tempted to be abusive to others, no matter how wrong we know it to be. Sometimes we can be strong and stable at one point in our lives, and in another set of circumstances, discover that we're weak and out of control. That doesn't mean we're evil—but when we feel like that, we need to seek help right away. If a person believes he might be predisposed to be abusive because of genetic make-up or family history, he too should seek help as soon as possible.

Organizations exist that can provide help for abusers. Domestic abusers or people who feel they are developing abusive characteristics should seek help from one of several organizations listed in the final chapter of this book—or look up a local program in the Yellow Pages. Getting help now could put an end for good to the vicious cycle of domestic violence.

condones violence against women"—but abusers often twist the sacred writings of various religions to suit their needs. When an abuser claims that God is on his side, it becomes much harder to argue with him!

In a similar way, abusive parents may quote scripture that praises obedience in children. However, being disciplined by your parents is not the same as being victimized by your parents. For example, if a guardian sends a child to his room for not doing his homework, she is probably looking out for the child's future, wanting him to do well in school. But if a

We often think of domestic violence as occurring only between adults. This graph, however, indicates a different reality: across the United States, by far the most incidents of domestic violence take place between children. This does not make the violence any less abusive or damaging. And the adults in the family are still the ones who are ultimately responsible for ensuring the safety of each member of the family.

caregiver hits a child for getting a B instead of an A on an exam, that is abuse. No religion teaches that God condones abuse!

Love

This one is perhaps the trickiest of all the reasons for staying in an abusive relationship. It's hard to walk away from someone you love, even if that person hurts you.

Often victims of abuse cling to a dream, the idea of the person they married, rather than the reality that exists today. Despite the abuse, these victims may hope against hope that their spouses or partners will go back to being the way they once were earlier in the relationship. They don't want to give up on

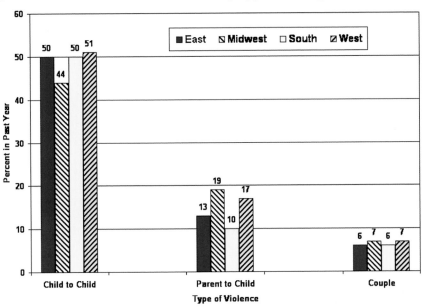

Abusive Violence by Type and Region

Are You in an Absive Relationship?

Do you:
- feel afraid of your partner or parent much of the time?
- avoid certain topics out of fear of angering your partner?
- feel that you can't do anything right for your partner or parent?
- believe that you deserve to be hurt or mistreated?
- wonder if you're the one who is crazy?
- feel emotionally numb or helpless?

Does your partner or parent:
- humiliate, criticize, or yell at you?
- treat you so badly that you're embarrassed for your friends or family to see?
- ignore or put down your opinions or accomplishments?
- blame you for his own abusive behavior?
- see you as property or a sex object, rather than as a person?

Does your partner or parent:
- have a bad and unpredictable temper?
- hurt you, or threaten to hurt or kill you?
- threaten to take your children away or harm them?
- threaten to commit suicide if you leave?
- force you to have sex?
- destroy your belongings?

Does your partner or parent:
- act excessively jealous and possessive?
- control where you go or what you do?
- keep you from seeing your friends or family?
- limit your access to money, the phone, or the car?
- constantly check up on you?

(Adapted from Helpguide.org.)

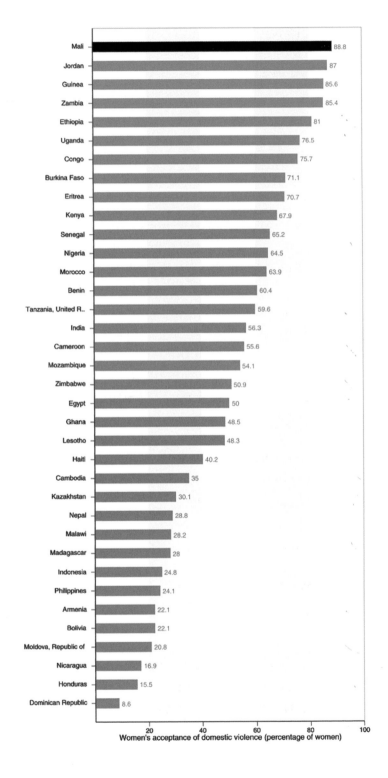

Country	Women's acceptance of domestic violence (percentage of women)
Mali	88.8
Jordan	87
Guinea	85.6
Zambia	85.4
Ethiopia	81
Uganda	76.5
Congo	75.7
Burkina Faso	71.1
Eritrea	70.7
Kenya	67.9
Senegal	65.2
Nigeria	64.5
Morocco	63.9
Benin	60.4
Tanzania, United R..	59.6
India	56.3
Cameroon	55.6
Mozambique	54.1
Zimbabwe	50.9
Egypt	50
Ghana	48.5
Lesotho	48.3
Haiti	40.2
Cambodia	35
Kazakhstan	30.1
Nepal	28.8
Malawi	28.2
Madagascar	28
Indonesia	24.8
Philippines	24.1
Armenia	22.1
Bolivia	22.1
Moldova, Republic of	20.8
Nicaragua	16.9
Honduras	15.5
Dominican Republic	8.6

Domestic violence is a worldwide problem. In some regions of the world, as this graph indicates, women accept it as a fact of life.

the people with whom they fell in love. Many times, victims may be emotionally dependent on their abusers; no matter how badly they are treated, they still feel they need their spouses or partners.

When children are the victims of abuse, their feelings are also often a mix of love and need. Children naturally love their parents. In some cases, abuse may seem normal to children because it's the only thing they've ever known; other children may hope that one day their parents will stop being abusive so they can be one big, happy family again.

In the case of elder abuse, the situation is reversed. Elderly parents often refuse to believe their children would ever take advantage of them. Instead, they blame themselves. It hurts too much to think that someone they love so much could let them down so terribly.

If you're looking in from the outside, you may wonder how any of the people in these situations could possibly love their abusers. But love isn't logical, and no one can tell another person whom to love—or whom not to love. Ultimately, however, victims of abuse must love *themselves* enough to choose to leave.

REALIZING THE TRUTH

In Weiss's own life, when she finally decided to leave her abuser, her reasons were none of the ones listed above. Instead, she simply—

finally—recognized the truth of her life. In *Surviving Domestic Violence: Voices of Women Who Broke Free*, she explained,

> During the eight years, seven months and twenty-one days of this abusive marriage, I never once realized that I was an abused woman . . . I never saw a pattern, because I never knew I should be looking for one.

Weiss, like many, was never taught that domestic violence can happen to anyone. She believed that domestic violence only happened to people who didn't look like her.

STORIES OF SURVIVAL

In this book, you will meet people who have each suffered through different forms of domestic abuse. They are real people and the events they describe really happened; these are not made-up, fictional stories (although all names and places have been changed to protect the individuals' identities). Each courageous individual who shared her story has learned from her experiences and has become a stronger individual because of them.

These women think of themselves not as victims but as survivors. They are neither sad nor weak. Even though their stories *are* sad, the individuals have learned from their experiences, and in many ways, they have risen above them.

Domestic abuse falls into a common pattern, or cycle of violence:

Abuse—The abuser lashes out with aggressive or violent behavior. The abuse is a power play designed to show the victim "who is boss."

Guilt—After the abusive episode, the abuser feels guilt, but not over what he's done to the victim. The guilt is over the possibility of being caught and facing consequences.

Rationalization or excuses—The abuser rationalizes what he's done. He may come up with a string of excuses or blame the victim for his own abusive behavior—anything to shift responsibility from himself.

"Normal" behavior—The abuser does everything he can to regain control and keep the victim in the relationship. He may act as if nothing has happened, or he may turn on the charm. This peaceful honeymoon phase may give the victim hope that the abuser has really changed this time.

Fantasy and planning—The abuser begins to fantasize about abusing his victim again, spending a lot of time thinking about what he or she has done wrong and how he'll make him or her pay. Then he makes a plan for turning the fantasy of abuse into reality.

Set-up—The abuser sets up the victim and puts his plan in motion, creating a situation where he can justify abusing him or her.

(Adapted from Helpguide.org.)

dissipate:
to cause to
spread thin
or scatter and
gradually
vanish.

activists:
people who
engage in
vigorous action
in support of
or opposition
to a particular
side of a
controversial
issue.

Unfortunately, however, the scars left by domestic abuse last a lifetime. Bruises and broken bones heal, but the psychological effects do not **dissipate** as easily. Each individual copes with these emotional scars in different ways. Some seek therapy or find trusted friends who will help them confront the pain of the past through talking about it; others attempt to leave their past in the past and avoid ever talking about their experiences. Still others choose to become **activists** and dedicate their lives to teaching people about domestic violence; they use their pain as a tool to help others.

The women who shared their stories for this book may each cope with her past in a different way—but all of them needed courage to tell their stories one more time. Some of them shared information they had never told even their loved ones. Divulging the darkest details of their pasts forced them to relive everything. As their voices described being choked by their husband, raped by their neighbor, or beaten by their father, their eyes and their trembling hands told their own story.

But they told their stories so that all of you out there reading this book will understand that domestic abuse is real—and it's happening right now all over the world, sometimes just next door, sometimes in your own home. These brave women didn't want anyone else to go through what they did. And they wanted

to say these words to all of you who are reading this book: "If you, or someone you know,
is the victim of domestic abuse, please find
help. No one deserves to be abused."

Chapter Two

SURVIVING SEXUAL ABUSE

When I walked into Maria Delgado's well-lit corner office, the first thing I noticed was the thick nameplate on her desk, an inky black rectangle with bold white letters. It didn't whisper, "maria delgado . . . um . . . superintendent?" Oh no, it downright demanded that everyone recognize: "MARIA DELGADO SUPERINTENDENT!"

Mrs. Delgado is a powerful woman. If you're a teacher, aide, or cafeteria worker at her school, she can get you fired if you don't do your job right. But don't worry, she is actually quite a friendly woman, well-liked by her staff. She is also an extremely diligent worker.

On the way to Maria Delgado's office, I had watched her walk purposefully through the hallways of her middle school. She spoke of the many aspects of the school for which she was responsible, as well as being the boss of many people. At just thirty-seven years old, she has rapidly climbed the professional ladder to success. Maria gets things done.

When I mentioned the nameplate, Maria's pride and passion for her profession was obvious in her response. "It is a tough job and often overwhelming," she said, "but I worked very hard to get here." She took extra courses in high school and graduated from college early at the age of nineteen. "I've always been a leader," she explained.

The second thing I noticed in the well-lit corner office stood directly to the right of

Rural Abuse

Some people are under the impression that rural areas are generally safer than urban areas. Sometimes this can be true, but as we have already discussed, domestic abuse is not picky and it can happen to anyone, anywhere. Abuse is as common in small farm-town communities as it is in bustling urban centers. And living in a rural area can present unique obstacles for the victims of abuse who live there. For example, if the rural community adheres to traditional family values, a victim of domestic violence who lives there may be less likely to leave her abusive partner because her community does not agree with divorce. Victims of domestic violence in rural areas may also have less access to shelters and organizations that can provide help. Many times, the family is located so far from town that no one ever sees what is happening, and the victim feels completely alone. This was the case with Maria Delgado.

the nameplate: a tiny Black Angus figurine. Maria looked a little embarrassed when I asked her about the miniature black cow, as though I'd caught her playing with a child's toy.

"I used to daydream a lot when I was a child," she said. "Actually, I used to fantasize and daydream until well into my twenties. And my favorite daydream of all was that one day I would own a great, big farm. I wanted to raise Black Angus cattle and show them nationally." She smiled at the figurine and explained that growing up on a farm, she had found great comfort in animals. "I trusted animals way more than people," she said.

When Maria was growing up, her family lived on a farm deep in the country. As a young child, her life had been peaceful and safe. She enjoyed the yearly and daily patterns of farm life, and she believed that bad things only happened far, far away. Then one day, her parents unintentionally invited the "bad things" to their home.

The farm was growing, and Maria's parents needed help; they decided to hire their neighbor John to work as a farmhand. John became a daily part of Maria's life. He brought with him a new and frightening world to Maria's once safe and isolated farmhouse, a world she and her family had never imagined.

Maria Delgado's neighbor, an employee of her parents, assaulted her sexually when she was eight. He was twenty-one. That first assault wasn't the end of it either; it turned

In a recent study, the U.S. Department of Justice's National Crime Victimization Survey found that 76 percent of sexually assaulted women were attacked by someone they knew well. Furthermore, when the perpetrators were friends or acquaintances, the rapes went unreported 61 percent of the time.

into a nearly decade-long campaign of sexual abuse that lasted until she was sixteen, when she left for college. Her family never knew what was going on.

"I can't really remember how it happened," she explained. "A comment or a small touch here or there eventually became sexual abuse. I didn't know why it was happening."

Maria described the confusion she felt; she did not understand what she had done to cause the abuse. It didn't make sense to her, and yet she was helpless to stop it. And as she grew older, John was not the only man who abused Maria.

Her family occasionally allowed hunters to stay overnight at their farm; these men also abused Maria, sometimes with words, sometimes with actions. Maybe they heard from John that Maria "was available." Maybe John had taught Maria to respond to men in ways she wouldn't have otherwise. Either way, it wasn't Maria's fault. These experiences only added to Maria's confusion and pain.

Maria's sister may also have been a victim of sexual abuse from local farmhands and visiting hunters, but she and her sister have never spoken to each other about their experiences. Like many abuse victims, they each lived in an isolated, private world, even though the abuse took place in their own home. Neither child ever told her parents. To this day, Maria assumes her parents never knew what was happening under their roof.

Children cannot always differentiate between what specialists call a "good touch" and a "bad touch."

Examples of a "good touch" include:

When someone you know and trust pats you on the back when you did a good job or lets you cry on their shoulder when you are feeling sad. A good touch can be a hug or a kiss from your mom or dad. A good touch feels comfortable to you and comes from someone with whom you feel comfortable.

~

Examples of a "bad touch" include:

A bad touch is when someone touches you when you don't want him to. A bad touch can feel wrong or make you uncomfortable. A bad touch can come from a stranger or from someone you know and trust. If someone forcefully touches you when you tell them not to or someone forces you to touch them when you don't want to, that is a bad touch. If someone tells you to keep this touch a secret, that is also a bad touch and you should tell someone you trust about it.

The farm had once seemed to Maria like the most perfect place in the world. Now it became her prison. She no longer felt safe in her own home. As she grew older and the abuse continued, she came to dread being home alone. As much as possible, she escaped the farm by going for long walks; as often as she could, she slept over at her friends' houses. But for years, she never told anyone what was happening.

If you feel afraid to go home, talk to someone. If you know someone who seems afraid to go home, ask him why he feels that way. If he seems unwilling to talk about it, tell someone who can help, like a teacher or the school counselor.

When Maria remembers her middle school years, what she recalls most clearly is an overwhelming and ever-present feeling of worry. Many of her friends had not even begun to think about boys as boyfriends; some of them had begun to wonder if boys thought they were pretty. Maria had much greater concerns: she was scared she might be pregnant.

This worry was much too heavy for such a young girl, but Maria did not allow it to consume her entirely. Like many abuse victims, she was strong enough to find coping mechanisms. Even though she didn't know how to physically escape the abuse she endured, she used her imagination to create a world where she could be safe. More and more, she lived in her daydreams. "I became like a zombie," she said. "I was in another world. I would fantasize a lot and write stories in my head."

Another survival technique on which Maria relied was hard work. While some abuse victims may begin to fail in school as a reaction to their situation, others, like Maria, demonstrate another approach: they use school as a refuge. Maria became a straight-A student. School was a safe place, a place where she could excel and feel good about herself. As she grew older, she also realized that her only hope of escaping John was by leaving her home—and if she studied hard, she could graduate sooner.

Her success at school, however, also hid her problems from the rest of the world. Maria was the sort of kid who everyone assumed had everything together. "No one knew what was going on," Maria told me. "I had good grades. I participated in clubs and leadership roles. I was a very active student."

Finally, Maria mustered up the courage to tell someone what was happening. The first two men she told betrayed her trust: they took advantage of her **vulnerability**, and they too abused her sexually. She felt as though there was no one she could trust.

But Maria didn't give up. "I told lots of people. But most people didn't believe me because I was such a good student and an active kid. To them, I was too 'normal' to have been abused." No one wanted to believe Maria. Maybe it made them feel uncomfortable. Maybe it just didn't seem possible. It was easier for them to think she was making up stories, looking for attention, playing a game.

By the time she was a teenager, Maria was strong enough in herself to know she needed to reach out and find comfort somewhere. She finally found it in an unlikely place. Although no adult took her story seriously, she befriended a young boy at her school who had been physically abused. He understood what she was going through. His support and understanding made a difference in her

vulnerability: capable of being physically or emotionally wounded.

life, and Maria credits him with giving her the courage to resist her abuser for the first time.

When Maria graduated early from high school, according to plan, she could escape at last to college. "I just *had* to leave," she said. After nine long years of abuse, she was ready to begin her life again.

Before she left for college, Maria confronted her abuser about what he had done to her. To her amazement, John was baffled by the idea that he had done something wrong. He believed he had never done anything to her that was against her will. Their relationship had been **consensual**, in his mind, and now he seemed convinced he would one day marry her.

consensual: involving or based on mutual agreement.

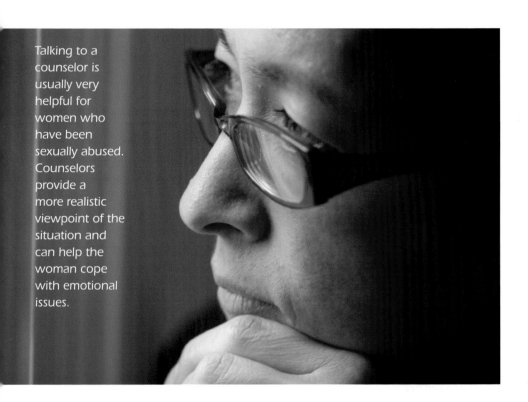

Talking to a counselor is usually very helpful for women who have been sexually abused. Counselors provide a more realistic viewpoint of the situation and can help the woman cope with emotional issues.

Maria's Survival Skills

Here is the advice Maria offers, based on what she learned from being sexually abused for nearly a decade during her childhood. Maria hopes that some of these skills may help you or someone you know.

- Tell someone, tell someone, tell someone. Tell someone you trust. If they turn out to not be trustworthy, tell someone else. Don't give up. You will eventually find someone who can help.
- You will put an end to the abuse when you are ready. Although it helps to have support, it is up to you to say, "Enough is enough!"
- Don't ever let your abuser tell you, "You asked for it." No one ever deserves to be abused. They are only trying to make you feel bad about yourself when they are the ones to blame.
- Work hard. Don't let your abuser stop you from achieving success. Your success shows your abuser that he or she does not have power over you.
- If you aren't ready to talk about your experience, try writing about it. This way, at least you are getting it off your chest and it may actually help you see more clearly what is happening to you, that you don't deserve it, and that you need to find help.
- Set goals for yourself. This will help you see that there is always a brighter future ahead of you and that one day you will be free of your abuser.
- If the domestic abuse you suffer is happening at one place in particular, even if it's your home, try to avoid that place. But you should also know that you should never live in fear. If you are afraid of a certain place or person, tell a counselor, a teacher, or someone you trust. You deserve to feel safe.

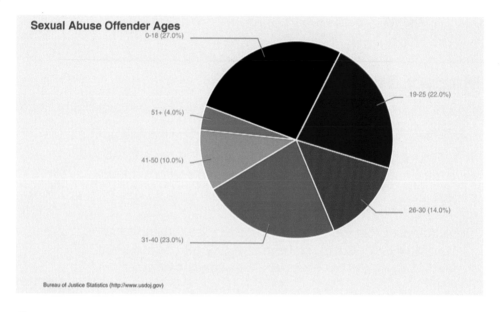

Sexual Abuse Offender Ages

- 0-18 (27.0%)
- 19-25 (22.0%)
- 26-30 (14.0%)
- 31-40 (23.0%)
- 41-50 (10.0%)
- 51+ (4.0%)

Bureau of Justice Statistics (http://www.usdoj.gov)

Contrary to stereotypes about "dirty old men," this graph from the U.S. Justice Department shows that most sexual abusers are younger men.

As a child, Maria had been too confused to understand what was happening, but by the time she was sixteen, she could see reality clearly: John had taken advantage of her for years and had sexually abused her. Now that she's an adult, she realizes John may have had psychological problems or a disorder that kept him from understanding his actions were wrong. But even if that were the case, it does not make the situation right, nor does it make Maria's pain go away.

Maria went on with her life; she was strong and determined to leave her past behind. In many ways she succeeded—but neverthe-less, her experiences shaped who she was as a young adult. Maria had been made aware of her sexuality at a very young age. Through no fault of her own, her experiences created habitual physical and psychological reactions.

Sexual abuse can make a woman feel "dirty" and ashamed, even though in reality she is not to blame in any way.

"The only way I knew how to get attention was sexually," she said, and she became sexually **promiscuous** at an early age. At college, sex became something she felt she could use, a **commodity**. It was something she could trade for something else, rather than a significant

promiscuous: not restricted to one sexual partner.

commodity: a product that has value.

Survivors of sexual abuse may feel as though a permanent shadow has been cast over their lives. However, people like Maria prove that abuse victims can take back their lives.

expression of feelings between two consenting individuals.

Although Maria continued to excel at academics, she was pregnant and married by the time she was eighteen. Despite this, Maria continued to take comfort in her goals for the future. Her ambitions were important to her; they gave her a sense of control over her life that she had never had as a child.

Today, Maria is a very successful woman. She has been married to the same man for nineteen years. In addition to her position as school superintendent, she also has the huge farm she always dreamed of owning. However, a decade's worth of sexual abuse did not just disappear from her mind once she achieved all her goals. Maria says her experiences are still a real part of who she is today; she believes they have harmed her—and also helped her.

On the one hand, trusting others is still very difficult for her. She has chosen to live her personal life far from town, and she keeps her children under close watch. Never once has she told her husband or her children anything about her abuse; she does not want them to know that such things are possible, that there are people out there who would do what John did to her. Maria also admits that these days her husband is sometimes verbally abusive to her, perhaps because she has become a strong, independent woman, unlike the quiet and submissive girl he met back in college, years ago.

Your body belongs to you and only you. No one should be allowed to touch it or force you to touch him or her against your will. You do not have to be physically touched to be sexually abused, either. If someone exposes him- or herself to you, makes sexual gestures, shows you sexual pictures, or even speaks to you in a way that makes you uncomfortable, get away fast and tell someone.

Children who are sexually abused are often intimidated. Their adult abusers often seem so powerful that children believe no one will believe them if they tell—or that they will suffer worse as punishment for telling.

On the positive side, however, Maria feels her experiences taught her compassion. Through them, she learned to pay attention to the small details that other people may miss. "It gave me a lens to the darker side," she said. "I know that homes that look perfect, aren't." As superintendent of a middle school, Maria tries to befriend her students, and she observes those around her carefully, watching for warning signs. She's ready to rescue students from the kind of horrors she endured as a child. "It makes me compassionate to others," she said, "and protective."

As Maria shared her story, she was clearly not asking for pity. She used her experiences as a motivation to work harder, do more, and to escape—but she didn't waste time feeling sorry for herself or becoming angry and bitter. "Anger hinders you," she said, "and lets [your abuser] have power over you." Maria refused to give her abuser the power to ruin her life. By becoming a successful woman, she feels she has proven to herself that she was better than he was. She has taken back the control he stole from her.

What's her advice for kids who are currently enduring any form of abuse? "Don't give up. Keep asking for help. Stand up for yourself." And most of all, find your Black Angus—whatever it is that will help you get through the pain in your life. "You will, eventually, get though it."

Chapter Three

SURVIVING CHILD ABUSE

Kathy Brown is the sort of person who looks like nothing bad has ever happened to her. She's a smiley woman who loves to eat the pies and cookies she bakes for her family. Her children and husband, her horses and dogs, and the small wallpapering business she runs all make Kathy a happy woman. "My life is good," she told me as we sat together at her kitchen table. She turned her coffee cup around and around, and took a deep breath; she looked like a woman who was getting up her nerve to face something frightening. "Hard to believe now what I lived with as a kid."

Kathy's father was a strict man who ruled his family with an iron hand. "It seemed like I couldn't do anything right when I was a kid," Kathy said. "He was always scolding me about something. Leaving my bike in the driveway. Making a mess in the kitchen. Letting the dog track mud into the house. It was never anything I meant to do wrong. Getting yelled at always took me by surprise. I'd be going along happy as you please—and the next thing I knew, I was in trouble."

Harsh scoldings weren't pleasant, but Kathy and her brother Kevin took them for granted when they were young. Her mother was a good-natured woman, and nothing much seemed to bother her. Kathy and Kevin learned to stay out of their father's way as much as possible. The two siblings were each other's best friends.

Then when Kathy was eleven and her brother was twelve, Kathy and her father had the biggest fight they'd ever had up until that point. "I don't even remember now what it was about," Kathy said. "All I know is I went running out, swearing I was never coming back. I went to a friend's house, and pretty soon I forgot all about it. We were having a good time, playing with Barbie dolls, when the phone rang."

Turned out Kathy's dad had sent Kevin after his sister. Kevin took his bike and went looking for her. He probably would have found her, too—after all, the brother and sister were close to each other and usually knew what the other was thinking—but he forgot to look as he was crossing the busy highway that ran through town. A truck hit him. The ambulance workers said he had been killed instantly.

According the Child Welfare Information Gateway, the following are indications of child abuse:

The child. . .
- shows sudden changes in behavior or school performance.
- has not received help for physical or medical problems brought to the parents' attention.
- has learning problems (or difficulty concentrating) that cannot be attributed to specific physical or psychological causes.
- is always watchful, as though preparing for something bad to happen.
- lacks adult supervision.
- is overly compliant, passive, or withdrawn.
- comes to school or other activities early, stays late, and does not want to go home.

The parent. . .
- shows little concern for the child.
- denies the existence of—or blames the child for—the child's problems in school or at home.
- asks teachers or other caretakers to use harsh physical discipline if the child misbehaves.
- sees the child as entirely bad, worthless, or burdensome.
- demands a level of physical or academic performance the child cannot achieve.
- looks primarily to the child for care, attention, and satisfaction of emotional needs.

The parent and child. . .
- rarely touch or look at each other.
- consider their relationship entirely negative.
- state that they do not like each other.

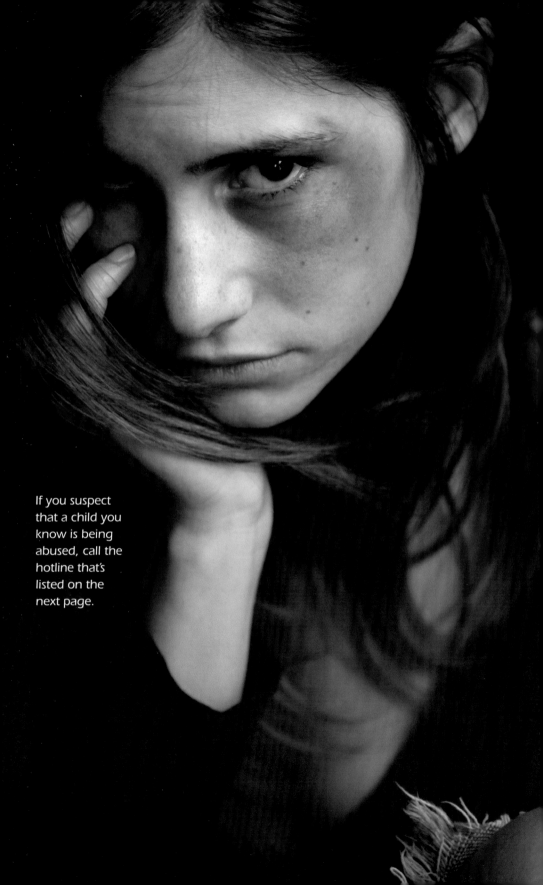

If you suspect that a child you know is being abused, call the hotline that's listed on the next page.

What to Do if You Suspect a Child Is Being Abused

Anyone can report suspected child abuse or neglect. Reporting abuse or neglect can protect a child and get help for a family—and it may even save a child's life. If you suspect a child is being abused or neglected or if you are a child who is being maltreated, contact your local child protective services office or law enforcement agency, so professionals can assess the situation. Many states have a toll-free number to call to report suspected child abuse or neglect. To find out where to call, consult the Information Gateway list at www.childwelfare.gov/pubs/reslist/rl_dsp.cfm?rs_id=5&rate_chno=11-11172.

Childhelp® is a national organization that provides crisis assistance and other counseling and referral services. Their hotline is staffed twenty-four hours a day, seven days a week, with professional crisis counselors who have access to a database of 55,000 emergency, social service, and support resources. All calls are anonymous. Contact them at 1.800.4.A.CHILD. (1.800.422.4453) or www.childhelp.org/get_help.

After that, life changed in the Brown household. Kathy's mother hardly ever spoke. Kathy blamed herself for her brother's death. And her father blamed her too. Or at least he said he did. "Now that I'm grown up," Kathy told me, "I wonder if he didn't blame himself really. But that was just too painful for him to face. So he took it out on me."

Where before her father had been prone to yelling when he got angry, now his anger

Every year, over 3 million children are reported for child abuse and neglect to child protective service (CPS) agencies in the United States. About 47 out of every 1,000 children are reported as victims of child maltreatment. Physical abuse represents 22% of confirmed cases, sexual abuse 8%, neglect 54%, emotional maltreatment 4%, and other forms of maltreatment 12%.

was violent. He punched a hole in the living room wall. He kicked the dog. He threw a plate across the kitchen. And then one day, he shoved Kathy so hard she fell down the stairs and broke her collarbone.

That was the first time it happened. Kathy's mother took her to the doctor and made up a lie about how she'd fallen out of a tree. Her mom never seemed to meet Kathy's eyes anymore, though, and Kathy decided her mother blamed her for Kevin's death too. "Maybe, I thought, Mom's glad Dad hurt me. And Dad never even said he was sorry."

After that, her father didn't get angry at Kathy for several months. He seemed to at least be trying to control his temper. But life was still dismal and gloomy in the Brown home, as though Kevin's death had sucked out all the things that had once made them a family. Everything seemed to go wrong. Kathy's father lost his job and had to go on unemployment. The furnace in their house broke, and they didn't have the money to fix it. Then the car broke.

Kathy came up behind her father while he was tinkering with the engine; her mother had asked her to call him in for supper. Maybe she startled him; she never knew for sure. All she knew was that he turned around and hit her with the back of his hand, so hard she remembers that she literally saw stars. Her ears rang for the rest of the evening.

For the next six years, Kathy learned to tip-toe around her father. She tried to fade into the walls; she didn't want to do anything to make him notice her, because if he noticed her, he was apt to hit her. "At first," Kathy said, "I genuinely believed I deserved it. I was so unhappy missing Kevin, and everything seemed so awful. It was like I didn't have a family at all anymore, just these strangers who didn't love me anymore."

As she grew into her teen years, though, Kathy started to get angry too. "I began to hate them, both my mom and my dad. I hated my father for hurting me all the time, I hated my mother for never protecting me. I would lie in bed at night and plot ways of getting even." Kathy stopped working in school, and her grades dropped—but her parents didn't seem to care. She stayed out late with her friends—but her parents never said a word. She began abusing alcohol and experimenting with drugs—but her parents didn't seemed to notice when she came home drunk or high. "I knew then that they really didn't love me," she said. "It was the loneliest feeling, to be fifteen years old and be pretty sure your parents don't care about you."

Luckily, a counselor at Kathy's school took an interest in her. Kathy talked to the counselor—and she also listened to what the counselor had to say. "It wasn't like I woke up one morning and it all clicked into place. It was just this gradual thing, that I slowly started figuring out that if my parents didn't care about me, then I had to care for myself.

Child abuse can be subtle. Sometimes it involves physical blows—and sometimes a constant barrage of emotional blows can also be abuse.

That I was only hurting myself with all the things I was doing. That it was time to take care of *me*."

When Kathy was seventeen, she moved out of her parents' house, dropped out of school, got a job at the mall, and got an apartment of her own. "I was ready to live my own life," she said. "I made a lot of mistakes—like not finishing school—but I don't really regret any of it. I was doing the best I could." Eventually, she earned her GED and went on to get an associate's degree at the local community college. She got married, had two children, got divorced, got married again, had another two children. And she never went to see her parents in all that time.

"One day, though, it hit me—I needed to forgive my mom and dad. If I didn't I was never going to be able to live my life the way I wanted to. I was still so angry inside. And sometimes I'd feel that anger waiting, like it was going to pop out any minute. It scared me. I didn't want to ever turn into my father. I didn't want to risk that I could hurt my own children the way I'd been hurt."

Kathy started going to a psychologist. She talked to her husband and her children about her childhood. She talked for hours to a good friend who listened and listened and listened. "She was almost as good as the counselor," Kathy laughed. "And I didn't have to pay her!"

Kathy eventually started visiting her parents again. "But we don't talk about the

Writing in a journal can be a good way to deal with the emotions and thoughts that child abuse leaves behind.

past. There just doesn't seem to be any point. Instead, whenever I feel the past creeping up on me, I write them long letters, letters I never send. Just pouring it out on paper seems to help."

What would Kathy tell a child who's being physically abused? "Don't think it's your own fault. No matter what you did, you don't ever deserve to be hurt. Children always deserve love. So if your parents are too sad or angry or sick inside to love you—well, then, you love yourself. Get help. Somewhere out there is an adult who can help you."

Chapter Four

SURVIVING DOMESTIC PARTNER ABUSE

Laura never thought of herself as the victim of abuse. Like many women who find themselves with an abusive partner, Laura just thought that her husband Gary had a particularly bad temper, the same way her dad did. And sometimes, when Gary got mad, he'd take it out on her. For a long time, it seemed pretty normal to her.

"It was normal for us for the man to abuse," Laura told me. "My dad would beat us all the time." It was also normal for Laura to see the "man of the house" doing a lot of drinking. So when Gary got drunk and began to hit her, Laura thought it was just something men did, something to be expected.

Laura and Gary had been girlfriend and boyfriend in high school. They got married when

Never Okay

Some victims of domestic abuse do not know that they are victims because they do not know the definition of abuse. Some victims think domestic abuse can only happen to certain people who fit a particular stereotype—be it geographic, ethnic, religious, or economic—but never to them. Other victims of domestic abuse do not know they are victims because they were raised in a domestically abusive household and it is all they know. Being raised in an abusive household does not mean you will definitely end up in an abusive relationship as an adult, but, as was the case with Laura, you may not realize that you do not have to be with someone who abuses you. Abuse is not normal and it is not okay.

they were very young, and Laura became pregnant. The "problem," said Laura, didn't start until after their first child was born. Although, come to think of it, she recalled, Gary had given her a pretty hard shove once when she was pregnant. . . .

But she hadn't thought anything of it. Even when Gary started hitting her, the abuse wasn't constant. For every six months of abuse, there would be six months of calm. She thought that was normal for a young married couple, just part of the ups and downs of marriage.

Laura can see now, however, that even before Gary's physical abuse began, from the very beginning he was psychologically abusive. Like most abusers, he found her weaknesses and poked at them. For instance, he knew she was ashamed of her upbringing, that she wondered whether she was "good enough" for Gary. Gary used this knowledge to whittle away at her self-esteem. He often told her she was from the "wrong side of the tracks" and that she should feel privileged to be with him. Because the things he said reinforced fears she already had, Laura mistook Gary's psychological abuse for the truth. *He's right,* she would think. *I don't deserve him. I need to "be on my best behavior" so as not to lose him.* Her belief that Gary was better than her made her willing to put up with his anger. Deep inside, a part of her believed she deserved it.

Until years after Laura left Gary, she did not fully understand all the ways her husband had been abusive to her from day one. "When you're in the middle of your life," she said, "it's often difficult to see clearly what's going on. With time and reflection, comes

Abuse and Pregnancy

According to the United Nations Population Fund, "About 1 in 4 women are abused during pregnancy, which puts both mother and child at risk." If your domestic partner abuses you in any way while you are pregnant, this is a major warning sign that they will continue to be abusive to you and that he also may abuse your child.

clarity. There's no point beating yourself up over knowledge you didn't have until later!"

After a few years of marriage and the birth of their first child, Laura could no longer avoid the reality: Gary's abuse had escalated from psychological to intermittent physical to intense physical abuse. His new favorite method of abuse was to choke his wife. Like many abusers, he always did it very carefully, making sure he never left a mark.

During one particularly traumatic act of violence, Gary raped Laura. When Laura

Anger and Abuse

A common misconception about abusers is that they just have bad tempers and should go to anger management classes. However, many abusers' actions are deliberate, intentional, and calculated. A man who supposedly "flew into a rage" would not be able to control where he hit his wife—and yet in most cases, the physical abuse is inflicted in areas the abuser knows can be easily hidden, such as the stomach, ribs, arms, or legs. According to Elaine Weiss in

Family and Friends' Guide to Domestic Violence:

Many abusers assault strategically, hurting their victims in ways that look accidental or leaving bruises that can be hidden by clothing. For example, victims report being burned with hot water, deliberate attacks that can easily be dismissed as clumsy kitchen accidents. They report being punched viciously and repeatedly in the abdomen, leaving huge bruises that vanish every morning when they dress for work. They report being strangled, which often leaves no bruises at all.

became pregnant as a result, Gary tried to force her to get an abortion. Laura refused—and Gary pushed her down the stairs, hoping to cause a **miscarriage**. Both Laura and the baby survived, but Laura was truly frightened now.

She was ready to end her marriage with Gary. When she tried to leave, though, he kidnapped their son Christopher and refused to give him back until Laura returned home. Fearing for the safety of her child, Laura believed she had no other choice but to return to her abuser.

Gary had been abusing alcohol for years, but later in the marriage, he turned to cocaine,

miscarriage: spontaneous expulsion of a human fetus before it is viable and especially between the 12th and 28th weeks of gestation.

Verbal, psychological abuse often escalates into physical abuse.

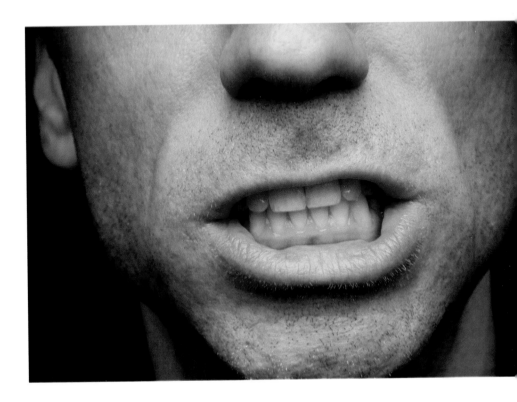

Rape Is Always a Crime

For many abusers, sexual abuse is seen as an effective way to both control and humiliate their victims. Some abusers declare that sex with their spouse is their "legal right," even if it is forced. Due to the psychological control abusers have over their victims, some victims are convinced that rape is okay if they are married or intimately involved with their rapist. According to the U.S. Department of Justice's Office for Victims of Crime, "A recently published eight-year study indicates that when perpetrators of completed rape are current or former husbands or boyfriends, the crimes go unreported to the police 77 percent of the time." Some victims feel ashamed or embarrassed to report being raped by their partner—but any forced sexual activity against a person's will is a crime.

LSD, and heroin. This combination of narcotics seemed to increase Gary's abusive behavior. Before long, he went from beating his wife to beating his children. During one incident, Gary grabbed his son Christopher by the throat, threw him across the room, and then demanded, "Get up and fight for yourself!" Laura was horrified.

Over the years, Laura had endured so much physical and psychological pain inflicted by her husband that she'd almost come to take it for granted. Now, however, when she witnessed her husband's attack on their son, something clicked in her brain. Maybe she hadn't loved herself enough to put an end to her own abuse—but she did love her children. She knew she had to leave.

For a long time, everyone who loved Laura had wanted her to leave her husband—but until now, she hadn't been ready. For many victims of abuse, a single turning point finally pushes them to say, "Enough, is enough!" Laura had reached that point: seeing her husband abuse their child was the final straw.

Laura left suddenly; she simply fled, without a plan. Gary found her all too quickly. He raped her, slammed her head against the ground, and drove off, leaving her in the middle of nowhere to fend for herself. Shaking, with little clothing, Laura walked along the

An abused spouse will sometimes take year after year of blows—and then suddenly find she has reached the turning point where she can finally walk away.

roadside, hiding in ditches whenever a car passed for fear that it might be Gary again. Despite what he had just done, however, despite her terror and loathing, she went back home, back to Gary. "To this day," she said, "I cannot explain my urge to go back to him. I figure that it's just an example of the psychological power he had over me at that time in my life."

The next day, Gary blamed her for the entire thing. "He said that because I tried to abandon him, I deserved exactly what I got."

Her head ached so badly from the beating he had given her that she eventually went to a doctor for help. When the doctor diagnosed a concussion, Laura found the courage to tell him that her husband was the one who had given it to her. The doctor gave Laura information about a domestic abuse program in the area. Laura began to carefully plan her escape.

First, though, she endured another six months of abuse alone before she was approved for a housing program for battered wives. With the organization's support and the help of her family, Laura left Gary for good and got her own apartment.

But Gary's abuse did not stop there. Because they lived in a small town, he soon discovered where Laura had moved. Furious, desperate to regain his control over her, he began stalking her. Because Gary's father

Laura's Warning Signs

Laura now plays an active role in watching for the warning signs of domestic abuse in others. Here is her list of warning signs that might indicate that a friend is experiencing abuse:

- Does your friend's boyfriend call your friend names or make fun of her in public?
- Has your friend started to wear long sleeves in warm weather, as though she might be hiding something?
- Has your friend suddenly stopped hanging out as much as she used to and doesn't seem to keep in touch with even her closest friends?
- Does your friend seem afraid to talk when her boyfriend is around?
- Has your friend given up doing things that she used to really love?

What you can do:

- Be a good friend and be ready to listen.
- Don't accuse or attack your friend's boyfriend. Just ask if things are okay and express that you are worried about her.
- If you feel like something is up but your friend is unwilling to discuss it, it may be time to tell an adult.

was the town's police chief, Laura didn't feel she could ask the local authorities for help. She knew Gary had spread rumors about her; some people in town believed Laura and Gary's marriage had failed because Laura had been unfaithful. They blamed her for the breakup.

Gary wanted Laura to know he was watching her; he wanted to make her afraid. Even if he couldn't hit her anymore, he still needed to feel he had control over her life. So he resorted to scenes straight from horror movies. One day, for instance, he broke into Laura's new apartment while she was showering and ripped open the shower curtain. He held a butcher knife over her head and laughed like a maniac. The next day at work, she received a dozen yellow roses, her favorite, with a card that read, "Almost."

In a household where spousal abuse is going on, it's not only the adults who are involved; innocent bystanders will also be hurt.

When Spousal Abuse Becomes Child Abuse

According to Elaine Weiss, "About half of abused women leave when the abuser physically or sexually assaults one of their children. But what mothers do not always realize is that even when children are not physically injured, it is emotionally devastating for a child to witness domestic abuse."

Gary continued to harass Laura for the next three years. Every day was a struggle for Laura as she worked to maintain a normal, healthy life for herself and her children. Gary refused to pay child support. Knowing he had the power to hurt her economically seemed to be almost as satisfying for him as hitting her. He didn't let go of her until he remarried—and found someone else to control.

For Laura, moving on wasn't as easy. Like many survivors of domestic abuse, she was reluctant to love and trust someone else; she was afraid of ever being that vulnerable again. She had no desire to date. "I felt like every man I met could be another abuser," she said. Besides, because she and Gary still lived in the same town, Gary easily kept tabs on Laura's actions. He'd been known to physically assault any man she so much as talked to. Laura took to telling men she was a lesbian so they would leave her alone.

After six years, Laura was finally ready to trust another man. She eventually remarried, and she has been married now for almost twenty years. Her second husband has never abused her. Laura's children have grown up, and today, they refuse to have contact with their father. Her daughter has become a domestic counselor who helps other women in abusive situations.

Meanwhile, Laura works in a school and does all she can to protect kids she thinks may be victims of domestic or social abuse. The rest of her time she spends doting on

Women who escape spousal abuse in time can go on to build strong and happy lives for themselves and their children.

her grandchildren. "It's always for someone else," she said. "The kids, but never for me."

Although in many ways Laura has grown and moved on, she still deals with the demons of her past. Like Maria and other survivors of domestic violence, Laura admits she is very defensive and finds it difficult to trust most people. She usually avoids social gatherings, especially if alcohol is involved; she doesn't have many friends or engage in any outside activities besides work. Instead, Laura focuses all her energy on the only people she feels she can trust: children.

"Sometimes," Laura said, "I wonder if it was all a dream. I don't feel like a victim anymore." She can barely imagine the young woman who walked away from an abuser twenty-five years ago. "These days," she said, "I'm a very feisty woman."

But back when she was married to Gary, leaving him was an action that seemed impossible to take. "You have to reach rock bottom," Laura said. "I saw that I was going to ruin my children's lives if I stayed. It was going to happen again, and the next time might be too late. In the end, I didn't escape for myself. I did it for the kids. If it were not for them, I might not have survived."

What's her advice to other people who find themselves in an abusive relationship? "Look beyond your current situation. If you are with someone who makes you feel bad about yourself, look outside—his opinion isn't the whole world's opinion."

Younger women can learn from the wisdom and experience of older women who have survived spousal abuse.

Talking with other people is the best way Laura has found to "look outside" herself. "When you keep your feelings bottled up inside," she said, "they can hide there inside you forever, where you can't see them. But the more you express your feelings about the things that happened in the past, the clearer and healthier you feel in the now."

Laura finds comfort in sharing her story with her children and grandchildren. She especially talks about her experiences with the girls in her family "to help them avoid ending up in a similar situation. Them knowing that this happens is better than growing up with blinders on. So if you've been abused, don't be afraid to tell your story. It's good for you—and it's good for others who might be in your same situation."

You may choose to share your experiences with one person you trust or with a whole group of people. You may choose to share your story in a private diary or at a national conference. The choice is completely yours.

Chapter Five
SURVIVING ELDER ABUSE

"The problem with survivors of elder abuse," says Kim Toot, director of the Allegany County Office for the Aging in New York State, "is that there are none."

Child abuse and intimate partner abuse are globally recognized issues. While there are still some people who would rather not admit that these forms of domestic violence happen within their own communities, published studies and statistics prove they are worldwide issues, as do the resounding voices of their victims. Women and children who have survived domestic abuse have written countless pages of autobiographies, anthologies, and Web sites, demanding to be heard. However, when it comes to the stories of elderly abuse survivors, the pages are suddenly missing.

So why don't elder abuse survivors tell their stories? According to Toot, there are three reasons:

- The victims of elder abuse do not realize they are being abused.
- They do not want to admit to being abused.
- They simply do not survive the abuse.

Consequently, the statistics for incidents of elder abuse are largely inaccurate, and abusive situations involving elders often go unchecked.

No one likes to think that someone they know could harm a frail old lady or a kindly old man. Of course, no one likes to think that anyone could hurt a child or a woman either. Human beings, even human beings we know, even ourselves, are capable of great cruelty to each other. Rather than ignore the truth, we must face it. As a culture, we need to go looking for signs of abuse; we need to protect those who are too weak to protect themselves—whether they're children or old people. As director of the Allegany County Office for the Aging, it is Kim Toot's job to do just that. It's a responsibility she takes seriously.

According to Toot, she and her organization look for five kinds of elder abuse.

1. NEGLECT AND SELF-NEGLECT

Neglect occurs when an elderly person does not receive the help he needs to care for himself. Self-neglect is the most common form of elder abuse and occurs when elderly individuals have lost the ability to take care of themselves or their surroundings. In describing her duties as director of the Office for the Aging, Toot explains that self-neglect is both

Self-neglect—the failure to care for yourself in all the ways you need in order to be healthy—is a common form of elder abuse.

the most common form of elderly abuse as well as the most difficult to determine.

Examples of Neglect

"I live with my daughter, but she's just too busy to prepare my meals. Now that I can't move around on my own, I spend most days feeling hungry. If she eats at home in the evenings, though, I can count on her sharing her supper with me."

"I just found out that my grandmother had no heat in her house most of this winter. Shouldn't my parents and my aunts and uncles do something to help her?"

"My neighbor is bedridden. He has a nurse who takes care of him, but today I discovered that he has bedsores from lying in the same position day after day."

Examples of Self-Neglect

"My dad has stopped bathing. He does not brush his teeth or wash his clothes anymore either. He used to be very well-groomed. I think he forgets to take care of himself now."

"My friend has recently stopped cleaning her house. She has never liked to throw things away, but it was at least somewhat orderly. Now there is stuff piled everywhere. I can barely find her in that mess!"

"Ever since my dad died, my mother won't make herself meals anymore. She's still healthy enough, she just doesn't seem to care. Sometimes when I go see her, she's so weak she can barely stand up. When I ask her if she's eaten that day, she says she can't remember."

Depression can play a role in an elderly person's self-neglect; they are simply too depressed to care enough to do the things necessary for normal daily life.

2. FINANCIAL ELDER ABUSE

This, the second-most common form of elder abuse, occurs when someone takes advantage of the victim's finances. This can include taking money (or possessions) from the victim without his knowledge or demanding money (or possessions) from a victim who is too weak physically and/or mentally to resist. Victims of financial elder abuse do not often report it, especially if a relative is the one who is victimizing them.

Examples of Financial Abuse

"I have recently looked over my father's doctor's bills and they seem outrageous to me! It looks like this doctor has been charging my father for care that he didn't even receive."

"My daughter makes me pay her bills for her. She is forty-five years old and unemployed. I feel bad for her and I want to help her, but she doesn't seem to even *try* to get a job and she makes me feel guilty if I do not give her money every month."

"I saw my cousin taking money from my grandmother's purse. When I said something about it to him, he said he does it all the time, and that she's too old to know the difference or even care."

3. SEXUAL ELDER ABUSE

Sexual abuse of an elderly person occurs when the victim is verbally, physically, or psychologically harassed in a sexual manner by another individual. This can include when an abuser touches the victim against her will, when an abuser forces the victim to touch him or someone else against her will, when an abuser forces the victim to watch him or others engage in sexual activity against her will, when an abuser exposes himself to the victim or speaks in a sexually inappropriate way to her, or when the abuser rapes the victim.

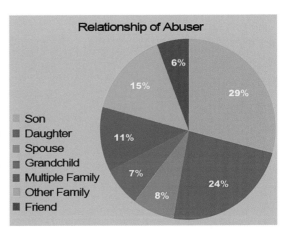

Relationship of Abuser

- Son
- Daughter
- Spouse
- Grandchild
- Multiple Family
- Other Family
- Friend

6%
15%
29%
11%
7%
8%
24%

Examples of Sexual Elder Abuse

"My mother's nurse has been watching pornographic videos while caring for her even though my mother has expressed to him that she doesn't like it."

"My son touches me in a way that makes me feel uncomfortable. He is my only caregiver and my son. I do not want to report him to the police."

"My daughter and her boyfriend have sex in the same room with me. When I

This graph indicates that sons and daughters are the most likely to be at blame in incidents of elder abuse.

ask her not to, she just laughs. It's almost like she enjoys knowing I'm there and there's nothing I can do about it."

4. PHYSICAL ELDER ABUSE

Physical abuse of an elderly individual is when the victim is physically harmed or

threatened by another individual. This can include (but is not limited to) when someone hits, scratches, shoves, kicks, slaps, bites, strangles, or otherwise causes physical harm to an elderly person. It also includes when an elderly person is threatened with physical harm. Physical elder abuse most often occurs at the hand of a caregiver (including a hired professional or a relative) who has become frustrated with caring for an elderly individual.

Examples of Physical Elder Abuse

"My grandfather's private nurse seems to be very rough with him. I have even noticed bruises on my grandfather's arms after his nurse has cared for him."

"My husband sometimes gets mad at me when I lose control of my bowel movements. He screams at me and throws things whenever it happens, but I can't help it."

"My daughter gets so frustrated with me when I do stupid things like leave the stove on or forget to close the back door. Yesterday, I forgot to turn the coffeemaker off and it burned a hole in the

Does One Form of Abuse Lead to Another?

Although no studies have definitively proved the link between abuse at one stage of life and another, some experts believe a victim of child abuse or spousal abuse is more apt to be a victim of elderly abuse.

Warning Signs of Elder Abuse

Malnutrition

When an elderly individual's weight drops significantly, the causes could be illness, lack of money for food, or simply that he is forgetting to eat. Forgetting to eat or go to the doctor when he's feeling ill could be signs of self-neglect, while the sudden lack of money for food might be a sign of financial abuse. Someone might be coercing the elderly individual into giving up his money, or someone may be taking the elder individual's money without his knowledge, leaving him with not enough funds to care for himself.

Shut-Off Notices

When an elderly individual has her utilities shut off, there could be several causes. If the individual is normally late with payments, it could just be a habit she has always had. If she has always paid her bills on time before, it could be a sign of self-neglect; she may be forgetting to pay her bills due to a developing disease such as Alzheimer's or another form of dementia. The third possibility is that someone is taking her money and she can no longer afford to pay her bills.

Bruises

Elderly people bruise easier than younger, healthier individuals, but not all bruises are merely a sign of aging or clumsiness. If you know an elderly person who has frequent, obvious bruising, it might be the result of abuse from his caregiver, spouse, or even his doctor. Physical abuse is not limited to a black eye. If someone is treating an elderly person roughly, including pushing, shoving, or grabbing him, these are all forms of physical elderly abuse.

Change in Appearance or Surroundings

Changes in housekeeping habits and personal hygiene may be symptoms of self-neglect. If an elderly person has an in-home caregiver, changes in appearance or surroundings may also be a warning sign that the caregiver may be abusive. Remember, neglect is also a form of abuse.

counter. When she found it, she gave me a shove so hard I fell down on the kitchen floor."

When an older person is made to feel ashamed or embarrassed, that is also a form of abuse.

5. PSYCHOLOGICAL/ EMOTIONAL ELDER ABUSE

This kind of abuse of elders happens when the abuser threatens, demeans, mocks, or humiliates the victim.

Examples of Psychological/ Emotional Elder Abuse

"I have heard my aunt's caregiver tell her that she wishes my aunt would die

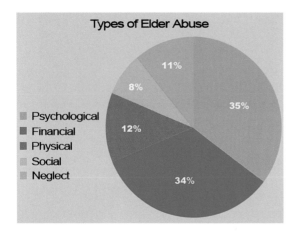

Types of Elder Abuse

- Psychological
- Financial
- Physical
- Social
- Neglect

11%
8%
35%
12%
34%

Financial abuse is one of the most common forms of elder abuse.

already. She tells my aunt that she hates taking care of her and that she is a burden to everyone."

"My daughter tells me that I am not capable of balancing my check book anymore, but I am. I always pay my bills on time and correctly and I've never bounced a check in my life. I still have all my wits about me, but it's like she's trying to convince me that I'm going crazy!"

"My husband makes fun of me when I forget things. He likes to point it out to everyone, like it's proof that I'm a stupid person now. I feel so humiliated."

A COMPLICATED PROBLEM

A common call that Toot receives in her offices goes something like this: "My next-door-neighbor has crap all over the place. I mean, he has piles and piles of junk in his backyard and on the front porch. And there are stray cats all over the property, too. It's a real eyesore in the neighborhood. Can you go in there and make him clean the place? It's just disgusting and I'm sick of looking at it."

For Toot, it's never as easy as just "going in there and making him clean the place." The elderly have the same rights as anyone else, including the right to private property. Although a neighbor may not like the look of a messy house next door, it is not illegal for an individual to accumulate "junk," so long as it does not stretch beyond property limits. "Hoarding" is one of the most common issues that confront **advocates** for the elderly, and it is a complicated one.

After receiving notification of possible self-neglect or other abuse, Toot's office must

advocates: people who defend the rights of another, or plead that person's cause or interests in a public forum.

According to the National Center on Elder Abuse 2005 fact sheet:

- Between 1 and 2 million Americans age 65 or older have been injured, exploited, or otherwise mistreated by someone on whom they depended for care or protection.

- Estimates of the frequency of elder abuse range from 2% to 10% based on various sampling, survey methods, and case definitions.

- Data on elder abuse in domestic settings suggest that 1 in 14 incidents, excluding incidents of self-neglect, come to the attention of authorities.

- Current estimates put the overall reporting of financial exploitation at only 1 in 25 cases, suggesting that there may be at least 5 million financial abuse victims each year.

Social workers and family members must distinguish between character traits and what is truly self-neglect. Old people are still entitled to be messy, just as young people are! But when messiness is a change in their personality, a more serious problem may be affecting them.

first assess the individual's "determining capacity." This means she and her staff use a series of questions and observations to determine whether the elderly individual is capable of making his own decisions. In the example given above, where the gentleman is hoarding possessions, the agency must determine whether his messiness is a result of self-neglect or is simply a character trait. In some cases, Toot explained, the elderly individual *always* kept a sloppy house and was a notorious hoarder, even as a younger person. In these cases, the agency has no right to interfere; if it decides that the individual has the determining capacity to make his own decisions about how he wants to live, then there is nothing the agency can do about his messiness! However, if the individual was not always a hoarder or a sloppy person, than his current messiness could be a sign that he needs in-home help, or even relocation to a facility for the elderly. It's up to Toot's office to listen and observe carefully, in order to make an accurate **assessment** of the situation.

The same fine line between self-neglect and just plain sloppiness exists in the matter of personal hygiene. When an elderly individual who was once clean and well-groomed begins to stop bathing, it may be a personal choice—or it may be that she is forgetting to bathe. If the elderly person is assessed as having the determining capacity to make her own decisions—after all, there's no law that says people have to take a shower every day!—then, again, agencies like Toot's have no right to interfere. It's a tough call to make sometimes.

assessment: determination of the importance, size, or value of a person or thing.

THE RIGHT TO BE ABUSED?

The line between self-neglect and personal choices may be difficult to see, but you might think Toot's job would be easier when it comes to other kinds of elder abuse, especially physical. However, Toot explained that this is not the case: even then, if the victim has the determining capacity to make decisions about her situation for herself, Adult Protective Services

(APS, a division of the Department of Social Services) can do nothing. "Sometimes," Toot said, "we get calls that an elderly woman is being abused by her husband. Sometimes we can refer the case to APS and they can get her out of the situation. And sometimes, there's nothing any of us can do about it." If the APS determines that the woman is "in her right mind" and can make her own decisions, then it is legally her choice to stay. In cases such as these, APS can do no more than declare that it is the elderly woman's rightful choice to stay with her abusive husband, meaning the agency must stay out of it. Some elderly women have been abused their entire married life and do not see themselves as victims. A grown adult in a domestically abusive situation cannot be forced to leave. Adult Protective Services can only step in under the following three circumstances:

1. If the elderly individual does not have the determining capacity to care for himself or herself.

2. If the elderly individual has no family or friends who can help him or her.

3. If the elderly individual is in imminent danger of hurting him- or herself or others.

THE SHAME OF ABUSE

At the Department of Social Services in Rochester, New York, I spoke with an elderly

Older people are sometimes dismissed as being not as valuable or as worthy of respect as other members of society. However, even when old people may not be practicing some of the elements of personal hygiene, their privacy must still be respected.

Older relatives need love and understanding, just as younger ones do.

woman named Tamara who was struggling to cope with life in the midst of the aging process. Tamara was an immigrant from Russia who had never learned to speak English well. As she aged, she was also losing her hearing, which made her feel even more isolated from the rest of the world. Her tone of voice told me she was angry and scared, but she had difficulty expressing her fears. She was obviously a proud woman who hated to admit weakness.

"The boys in her apartment building have been stealing from Tamara," her APS worker told me. "They're relatives of hers—grand-nephews and great-grandsons—but they don't like her, because she's been yelling at them since they were little. So they take the money from her purse, the food from her refrigerator, even one time her shoes out of her closet. They think it's funny. Poor Tamara doesn't know what to think. She doesn't know if she's losing her mind. She hates to even talk about it. She's just too proud. She's terrified her family is going to put her in a nursing home, so she'd rather not talk too much about her problems."

Many elderly individuals feel ashamed of their situation. Getting old is a complicated and difficult experience. When we see an old woman like Tamara with white hair and a wrinkly face, we forget she was once a child, a teenager, a young woman, a strong adult—but the old woman remembers. Aging means giving up so many things: our physical strength, our sense of ourselves as contributing members of society, and hardest of all, our independence. As a result, sometimes when an elderly individual is being abused, she would rather not admit it to others or even to herself. She's afraid the abuse will make

It's difficult to take care of a senior when he or she has many different needs, and it's difficult to be elderly when age brings with it infirmities and dependence. Both the demands of caregiving and the needs of the elder can create situations in which abuse is more likely to occur.

others see her as weak, that it will mean she has to give up whatever independence she has left.

Feelings of shame can be even worse if a family member or a loved one is abusing the elderly person. For example, many victims would rather help their sons or daughters by paying their bills every month than admit that their own children are financially abusing them. Even if an elderly person is being physically abused, he may not want to get his child or other loved one into trouble by reporting the situation.

Pride and embarrassment can play a role in an older person's unwillingness to seek help.

WE'RE ALL GOING TO BE OLD!

Prejudice is often caused by ignorance: We don't understand a particular culture, and so we make assumptions about the people who come from that culture. Or we assume that people who look a certain way all act a certain way. We think that people who worship God differently from ourselves are scary and evil. We've never walked in the other person's shoes, and we probably never will. All we can do to dispel our ignorance and smash our prejudice is try to learn more about other points of view. But when it comes to prejudice against the elderly, one day—if we're

Young and old are not so different! We all can benefit from another's love and support.

lucky!—we're all going to have the chance to find out what it's like to be old.

Some cultures value old people. They see them as sources of wisdom. They appreciate the fact that age doesn't take away what a person has to give—and in many cases, age enriches a human being. But North American mainstream culture tends to look down on the elderly. We dismiss them as too weak, mentally and physically, to be able to contribute much.

As a result, all too often the signs of abuse are read simply as signs of aging. Our culture has concluded that when people get older, they begin to "lose their train of thought." This is normal, we tell ourselves. But in reality, confusion and the loss of memory are not normal signs of aging; they are warning signs of impending conditions such as Alzheimer's and other forms of dementia. To chalk up these conditions to "just getting older" is neglectful. Illness, injury, and depression are not normal conditions for the elderly either. These too can be signs of abuse.

The elderly deserve their rights as much as anyone else. They deserve to be loved, respected, and cared for, just as our children do. The elderly carry in their minds our history, and they can enrich us with their wisdom. And we should never forget: one day, we will be the elderly!

Risk factors for elder abuse

Many nonprofessional caregivers — spouses, adult children, other relatives and friends — find taking care of an elder to be satisfying and enriching. But the responsibilities and demands of elder caregiving, which escalate as the elder's condition deteriorates, can also be extremely stressful. The stress of elder care can lead to mental and physical health problems that make caregivers burned out, impatient, and unable to keep from lashing out against elders in their care.

Among caregivers, significant risk factors for elder abuse are
- inability to cope with stress (lack of resilience)
- depression, which is common among caregivers
- lack of support from other potential caregivers
- the caregiver's perception that taking care of the elder is burdensome and without psychological reward
- substance abuse

Even caregivers in institutional settings can experience stress at levels that lead to elder abuse. Nursing home staff may be prone to elder abuse if they lack training, have too many responsibilities, are unsuited to caregiving, or work under poor conditions.

(Source: Helpguide.org)

Chapter Six

WHAT TO DO IF YOU OR SOMEONE YOU KNOW IS BEING ABUSED

If you or someone you know is being abused, here's the most important thing: tell someone, tell someone, tell someone! It could make all the difference in the world.

Included here is a list of organizations that can help victims of domestic abuse. You can also look up local shelters and programs in your local Yellow Pages.

FOR VICTIMS OF CHILD OR TEEN ABUSE

If you are a child or teen being abused, tell someone you trust.

If you are or someone you know is in immediate danger, call 911.

Families should
work together
to keep each
other safe.

You can call this number for help: the Childhelp National Child Abuse Hotline at 1-800-4-A-CHILD (1-800-422-4453).

FOR VICTIMS OF INTIMATE PARTNER ABUSE

If your domestic partner is abusing you, tell someone you trust. If you are in immediate danger, call 911.

If you are worried that someone you know is being abused by her domestic partner, talk to her first. If she is in immediate danger, call 911.

If you are being domestically abused and are ready to leave your abusive partner, you need to plan your escape so that you are not in danger immediately after leaving. If you have someone you can trust, tell him or her that you are planning to leave and ask for his or her assistance.

Call the following number for help planning your escape or to find a shelter immediately (if your partner monitors your phone calls, use a payphone, a public phone, a doctor's phone, or a friend's phone): *National Domestic Violence Hotline* at 1-800-799-7233 (SAFE), or 1-800-787-3224 for the hearing impaired. You can also reach them by e-mail at ndvh@ndvh.org. (If your partner tracks your computer use, use a public library or school computer, or the computer of a trusted friend.) More information can be found at *The National Domestic Violence Hotline* Web site at www.ndvh.org.

FOR VICTIMS OF ELDER ABUSE

If you or someone you know is in immediate danger, call 911.

If you are an elder who is being abused, tell someone you trust.

If you know an elder who is being abused, call Eldercare Locator at 1-800-677-1116.

FOR ABUSERS WHO WANT TO STOP

If you are abusive, have been abusive, or fear you may become abusive and you want help, you can contact any of the above numbers or look up a local program in the Yellow Pages.

THE MOST IMPORTANT THING TO REMEMBER

Tell someone! Once you do, the situation can change. It takes courage—but there are people who can help survivors of abuse go on to live safe lives.

Abuse is a secret that should never be kept.

Better Ways to Approach a Possible Victim of Domestic Abuse

Don't make generalizations. Cite a specific incident. For example:

> "I heard Tim call you 'stupid' in front of everyone last night. That seemed to hurt your feelings."

> "You seemed scared of your dad yesterday when I was at your house. Why is that?"

> "I've noticed bruises on your arms after you come home from the doctor. Is he hurting you?"

Don't blame the person or try to make him or her feel guilty for changes in personality or social life. Instead, try:

> "I really miss hanging out with you. Is there a reason we don't hang out much anymore? I would really like to."

> "I've noticed you seem to be thinking about something else most of the time lately. Is there anything we could talk about that would help you feel better?"

Don't threaten to harm the abuser. It is likely that the victim wants to protect her abuser and if you threaten to hurt him, she will not trust you enough to talk to you about what is going on. Just express your concern without threats:

"I am worried about you. How are you?"

Don't make the victim feel stupid for being in an abusive relationship. Remember, it can happen to anyone and the victim is most likely in a weakened psychological state. Again, just try to express your care and concern:

"I am always here for you, if you ever want to talk. I want to know that you are okay because you are important to me."

Don't make threats. If you are worried that someone is being abused, talk to the person first. You could possibly make the situation worse by alerting authorities if the victim is unwilling to cooperate. Instead try something like,

"I have seen the way your parent/guardian/caretaker/ partner treats you and it is wrong. Do you want to talk to someone about it? I am worried about you."

However, if this person's life is in immediate danger, then you should tell someone right away. Call 911.

If You're Still Living in an Abusive Home

(Things You Can Do to Help Keep You Safe)

Know your abuser's red flags. Be on alert for signs and clues that your abuser is getting upset and may explode in anger or violence. Come up with several believable reasons you can use to leave the house (both during the day and at night) if you sense trouble brewing.

Identify safe areas of the house. Know where to go if your abuser attacks or an argument starts. Avoid small, enclosed spaces without exits (such as closets or bathrooms) or rooms with weapons (such as the kitchen). If possible, head for a room with a phone and an outside door or window.

If you're an adult, be prepared to leave at a moment's notice. Keep the car fueled up and facing the driveway exit, with the driver's door unlocked. Hide a spare car key where you can get it quickly. Have emergency cash, clothing, and important phone numbers and documents stashed in a safe place (at a friend's house, for example).

Practice escaping quickly and safely. Rehearse your escape plan so you know exactly what to do if under attack from your abuser. If you have children, have them practice the escape plan also.

Come up with a code word. Establish a word, phrase, or signal you can use to let your children, friends, neighbors, or co-workers know that you're in danger and the police should be called.

Make and memorize a list of emergency contacts. Ask several trusted individuals if you can contact them if you need a ride, a place to stay, or help contacting the police. Memorize the numbers of your emergency contacts, local shelter, and domestic violence hotline.

Keep change and cash on you at all times. Know where the nearest public phone is located, and have change available so you can use it in an emergency situation to call for help. Also try to keep cash on hand for cab fare.

Additionally, to keep yourself safe from domestic abuse and violence you should document all abuse. If you've been injured, take photographs. If you have been abused in front of others, ask witnesses to write down what they saw. Finally, don't hesitate to call the police if your abuser has hurt you or broken the law. Contact the police even if you just think your abuser might have broken a law. Assaulting you, stealing from you, and destroying your property are all crimes.

(Adapted from Helpguide.org.)

Further Reading

Burns, Kate, ed. *Current Controversies: Violence Against Women*. Farmington Hills, Mich.: Greenhaven Press, 2008.

Curry, Shaunelle. *Shairi's Journey: Through Darkness into Light*. Victoria, British Colombia: Trafford, 2006.

Dawes, Cheryle. *Domestic Violence: Both Sides of the Coin*. Victoria, British Colombia: Trafford, 2006.

DelTufo, Alisa. *Domestic Violence for Beginners*. Denbury, Conn.: Writers and Readers, 2005.

Freed, Kecia. *I Wish the Hitting Would Stop*. Fargo, N.D.: Rape and Abuse Crisis Center, 2002.

Weiss, Elaine. *Family and Friends' Guide to Domestic Violence: How to Listen, Talk and Take Action When Someone You Care About is Being Abused*. Volcano, Calif.: Volcano Press, 2003.

For More Information

Administration on Aging
www.aoa.gov/index.asp
Administration on Aging site with information about their mission, budget, and organizational structure, as well as the Older Americans Act.

Center for Disease Control and Prevention
www.cdc.gov
The federal government's online source for credible health information.

Helpguide
www.helpguide.org
A free, non-commercial resource for people in need, Helpguide's mission is to empower people to understand, prevent, and resolve health challenges.

Men's Network Against Domestic Violence
National Programs
www.menagainstdv.org/action/
    national-programs.html
This organization works to increase men's involvement in programs and efforts that will prevent domestic violence.

National Adult Protective Services Association
www.apsnetwork.org
A forum and resource for sharing information, solving problems, and improving the quality of services for victims of elder and vulnerable adult abuse.

For More Information

National Center on Elder Abuse:
Administration on Aging
www.ncea.aoa.gov/NCEAroot/Main_Site/
  Index.aspx
A national resource center dedicated to the prevention of elder mistreatment, abuse, neglect, and exploitation.

The National Domestic Violence Hotline
www.ndvh.org/index.php
Helpful site where visitors can gather information about domestic violence and about what the National Domestic Violence Hotline does to help women, children, and men who are in abusive relationships.

Office for Victims of Crime
www.ojp.usdoj.gov/ovc/
Established by the 1984 Victims of Crime Act (VOCA), the Office for Victims of Crime (OVC) oversees programs that benefit victims of crime. Their site provides details about funding for state victim assistance and compensation programs as well as training programs designed to educate criminal justice and allied professionals regarding the rights and needs of crime victims.

Prevent Child Abuse America
www.preventchildabuse.org/index.shtml
Resource for anyone wanting to learn more about efforts to prevent the abuse and neglect of children in the United States. Site includes

information about local programs, prevention initiatives, and events.

U.S. Department of Health and Human Services
www.hhs.gov
Government site with comprehensive information regarding improving the health, safety, and well-being of Americans.

The United Nations Population Fund
www.unfpa.org
Site for the international development agency that promotes the right of every woman, man, and child to enjoy a life of health and equal opportunity.

World Heath Organization
www.who.int/en
As the directing and coordinating authority for health within the United Nations system, the WHO's site provides information on global health matters. Data and statistics are available for all WHO member countries.

Publisher's note:
The Web sites listed on these pages were active at the time of publication. The publisher is not responsible for Web sites that have changed their addresses or discontinued operation since the date of publication. The publisher will review and update the Web-site list upon each reprint.

Bibliography

Burns, Kate, ed. *Current Controversies: Violence Against Women*. Farmington Hills, Mich.: Greenhaven Press, 2008.

Carnot, Edward J. *Is Your Parent in Good Hands? Protecting Your Aging Parent from Financial Abuse and Neglect*. Herndon, Va.: Capitol Books, 2004.

Johnson, Jerry L. and George Grant. *Casebook: Domestic Violence*. Columbus, Ohio: Allyn & Bacon, 2004.

Mellor, M. Joanna, and Patricia Brownell, eds. *Elder Abuse and Mistreatment: Policy, Practice, and Research*. Binghamton, N.Y.: The Haworth Press, 2006.

Richie, Beth E., Natalie J. Sokoloff, and Christina Pratt. *Domestic Violence at the Margins: Readings on Race, Class, Gender, and Culture*. Piscataway, N.J.: Rutgers University Press, 2005.

Sandell, Diane S., and Lois Hudson. *Ending Elder Abuse: A Family Guide*. Fort Bragg, Calif.: QED Press, 2000.

Weiss, Elaine. *Family and Friends' Guide to Domestic Violence: How to Listen, Talk and Take Action When Someone You Care About is Being Abused*. Volcano, Calif.: Volcano Press, 2003.

Weiss, Elaine. *Surviving Domestic Violence: Voices of Women Who Broke Free*. Scottsdale, Ariz.: Agreka Books, 2000.

Wilson, K.J. *When Violence Begins at Home: A Comprehensive Guide to Understanding and Ending Domestic Abuse*. 2nd ed. Alameda, Calif.: Hunter House Publishers, 2006.

Index

Picture Credits

Dreamstime
- Absolut Photos: p. 84
- Bellanordi: p. 86
- Corot2: p. 42
- Costa007: p. 112
- Isatori: p. 110
- Jklune: p. 70
- Kozikowsk, Piotr: p. 56
- Loutocky, Tomas: p. 54
- Madmaxer: p. 114
- Maszas: p. 107
- Muellek, Josef: p. 103
- Nuzzaco, Christopher: p. 68
- Palangsi: p. 58
- Puentes, Alexis: p. 12
- Russell, Jennifer: p. 32
- Sánchez Reye, Jose Antonio: p. 53
- Shado59: p. 100
- Viviolsen: p. 8
- Yanc: p. 97

iStockphoto: p. 15, 62, 66
- Bendjy, Daniel: p. 82
- Bernardino, Eduardo Jose: p. 106
- de Haas, Anne: p. 91
- De Suza, Brendon: p. 30
- Foley, Steven: p. 80
- Friedman, Rob: p. 50
- Geotrac: p. 16
- Hood, Eric: p. 75
- Horrocks, Justin: p. 29
- Kemter, Michael: p. 25
- Papas, Mark: p. 89
- Pelletier, Marcel: p. 77
- Perkins, Thomas: p. 10
- van Caspel, Wouter: p. 104
- Young, Lisa F.: p. 94

Jupiter Images: p. 10

About the Author and the Consultant

Author
Joyce Zoldak lives in New York City and works for the nonprofit sector. She will be pursuing a master's degree in Urban Policy in fall 2009.

Consultant
Andrew M. Kleiman, M.D. is a Clinical Instructor in Psychiatry at New York University School of Medicine. He received a BA in philosophy from the University of Michigan, and graduated from Tulane University School of Medicine. Dr. Kleiman completed his internship, residency, and fellowship in psychiatry at New York University and Bellevue Hospital. He is currently in private practice in Manhattan and teaches at New York University School of Medicine.